- 4 MAR 2017

2 4 APR 2018

WRN

Renewals

0333 370 4700

arena.yourlondonlibrary.net/
web/bromley

Bromley

THE LONDON BOROUGH
www.bromley.gov.uk

Please return/renew this item
by the last date shown.
Books may also be renewed by
phone and Internet.

Little Pebble™

Celebrate Spring
Rain Showers

by Kathryn Clay

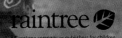
raintree
a Capstone company — publishers for children

Raintree is an imprint of Capstone Global Library Limited, a company incorporated in England and Wales having its registered office at 264 Banbury Road, Oxford, OX2 7DY – Registered company number: 6695582

www.raintree.co.uk
myorders@raintree.co.uk

Edited by Erika L. Shores
Designed by Juliette Peters and Ashlee Suker
Picture research by Svetlana Zhurkin
Production by Katy LaVigne
Originated by Capstone Global Library
Printed and bound in China.

ISBN 978 1 4747 1236 1

19 18 17 16 15
10 9 8 7 6 5 4 3 2 1

British Library Cataloguing in Publication Data
A full catalogue record for this book is available from the British Library.

Acknowledgements
We would like to thank the following for permission to reproduce photographs: iStockphoto: dennisjim, 9; Shutterstock: Aspen Photo, 15, Brian A. Jackson, 5, Gayvoronskaya_Yana, 7, Geo Martinez, 20, georgemphoto, 11, Maksim Chaikou, 1, Marten_House, 19, Olha Ukhal, 3, Patrick Foto, cover, Photo Fun, 17, Stacey Ann Alberts, 21, tab62, 13, USBFCO, back cover and throughout.

Every effort has been made to contact copyright holders of material reproduced in this book. Any omissions will be rectified in subsequent printings if notice is given to the publisher.

All the internet addresses (URLs) given in this book were valid at the time of going to press. However, due to the dynamic nature of the internet, some addresses may have changed, or sites may have changed or ceased to exist since publication. While the author and publisher regret any inconvenience this may cause readers, no responsibility for any such changes can be accepted by either the author or the publisher.

Contents

Spring is here! 4

Rain helps plants 10

Rain helps animals 14

After a storm 18

Glossary 22
Find out more 23
Websites 23
Index 24

Spring is here!

Winter is over.

The days grow warmer.

Rainy spring weather is here.

Dark clouds roll in.

Lightning flashes.

Boom! Thunder bangs.

Tiny drops start to fall.

Heavy showers soak the ground.

8

Rain helps plants

Roots suck up the rain.

Stems poke from the soil.

Leaves grow on the stems.

Flower buds grow.

Soon pink tulips bloom.

Rain helps animals

Rain makes puddles.

A thirsty deer takes a drink.

Worms die if they dry out.
Rain keeps their bodies wet.

After a storm

Poppy puts on boots.

She plays in the puddles.

The Sun comes out.

James sees a rainbow.

21

Glossary

bloom   produce a flower

bud   part of a plant that turns into a leaf or flower

root   part of a plant that attaches to the ground

stem   main body of a plant

Find out more

All About Flowers (All About Plants), Claire Throp (Raintree, 2014)

Everything Spring (Picture the Seasons), Jill Esbaum (National Geographic Society, 2010)

What Can You See in Spring? (Seasons), Sian Smith (Raintree, 2014)

Websites

discoverykids.com/articles/how-do-rainbows-form
Find out how a rainbow forms.

easyscienceforkids.com/all-about-rain
Learn fun facts about rain on this website.

www.bbc.co.uk/education/clips/zhfnvcw
Watch the changing of the seasons in this video.

Index

buds 12

clouds 6

deer 14

leaves 12
lightning 6

puddles 14, 18

rain 4, 8, 10, 14, 16
rainbows 20
roots 10

showers 8
stems 10, 12
Sun 20

thunder 6
tulips 12

weather 4
winter 4
worms 16